A Helping Hand

Written by
Rob Waring and **Maurice Jamall**
(with contributions by **Julian Thomlinson**)

Before You Read

to bark

to bite

to ride

beach
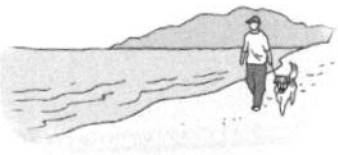

blood
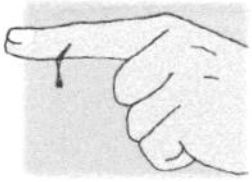

dolphin

footprints

gate

hill

land
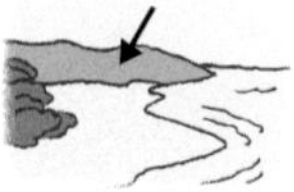

map
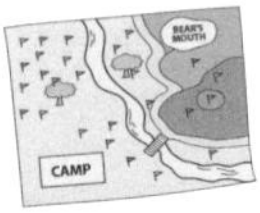

mouth
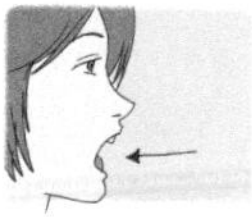

path

signs

dark

nervous

In the story

David

Daniela

Tyler

Mr. Jenkins

"It's this way, I think," said David. He was with his friends, Daniela and Tyler. They were going to the beach on their bikes. Daniela was taking a picture of the beach.

"I love this place," she said. "This is going to be fun."

David started riding up the hill. "Slow down, David," said Daniela. "It's not a race!"

"What's the plan? Which beach are we going to?" asked Tyler.

"Jenkins Beach," said David.

"Jenkins Beach?" said Daniela. She was not happy. "No way! I'm not going there. It's too dangerous."

Tyler said, "What are you talking about, Daniela?"

"Don't you know?" said Daniela. "It's near old Mr. Jenkins's house. Everybody hates him."

"But why?" asked Tyler.

"He's got lots of dogs, big, angry dogs," Daniela continued. "If we go on his land, the dogs will come and bite us."

"Why doesn't he want people on his land?" asked Tyler.

"Nobody knows," said Daniela. "But he doesn't want people on his land. Everybody stays away from him and his dogs."

"Is that Mr. Jenkins's house?" asked Tyler. He was pointing at a house on a hill.
"Yes, that's right," said Daniela. "It's best we don't go near. We don't want his dogs to bite us."
David said, "It doesn't look like a very friendly place."
Tyler replied, "It's okay. You don't need to worry."
Daniela said, "Let's not go to Jenkins Beach. Can we go to Seaview Beach?"
"Great idea! Let's go," said David.

They rode their bikes up the hill. It was a long way and soon they were tired. They came to two paths.
"Is this the way, David?" asked Daniela. She pointed down the hill.
"Yes, I think so," he replied. "It's my first time here, so I'm not sure. Which one do we take? Tyler, you're good with maps."
Tyler looked at the map. "I think it's this way," he said, pointing to the path up the hill. "But the map says the path goes near Mr. Jenkins's land."
"That's okay," said David. "If it goes near his land, but not on it, we'll be okay."

They went up the hill. Soon they came to a gate. It was the gate to Mr. Jenkins's land and the way to Jenkins Beach. There were signs near the gate.

"Oh, this is the wrong path. I don't want to go back, let's go to Jenkins Beach," David said.

"No, David! Stop!" said Daniela. "Let's go a different way. Can't you read? Don't you understand? It says *Dogs. Keep out*! Don't go near there, David!"

"Stop worrying," said David. "I like dogs. And dogs like me. It'll be okay."

Then Daniela heard one of the dogs. "I can hear one of the dogs. Don't go that way, David!"

"Don't worry, Daniela," Tyler replied.

David and Tyler did not listen. They rode their bikes through the gate. Daniela followed behind them. She was nervous. She did not like dogs.

Tyler said to David, "Come on, David. I'll race you to the beach. I'll win!"

"Okay, let's go," said David excitedly. The two boys started to race up the hill.

"Come on, Daniela," Tyler shouted.

"I'm not racing!" said Daniela. "You two can race. I don't want to. And don't shout, Tyler. The dogs will hear you. Be careful of the dogs. They're big and dangerous."

Tyler replied, shouting, "Hurry up, Daniela! We don't have time."

"Don't shout!" she replied.

David and Tyler were racing up the hill. It was a long way through the dark forest. They were going near old Mr. Jenkins's house.

Suddenly, Tyler stopped. He listened. "Can you hear that?"

"Can I hear what?" said David.

"That noise. There's something in those trees. Let's go carefully," said Tyler.

The boys rode their bikes slowly up the hill.

Daniela was pushing her bike up the hill. She was a long way behind them. Suddenly, Tyler and David came racing back down the hill. Daniela was very surprised.
"Dogs! Dogs! They're coming for us!" shouted Tyler.
"Big, angry dogs! Go, go!"
"What?" said Daniela. "Oh no. I told you!"
Tyler did not stop. He rode his bike quickly down the hill.
"Come on, Daniela! Let's get out of here!"

Tyler and Daniela raced down the hill on their bikes. They did not want to see the dogs. They were very scared. They could hear the dogs barking behind them. They did not look back.
As Daniela rode her bike, she dropped her bag. "My bag," she shouted to Tyler. "I dropped my bag!"
"Leave it!" said Tyler. "The dogs are coming."
Daniela and Tyler left the bag and raced down the hill.

Soon, Tyler and Daniela got off their bikes. "I told you not to go near old Mr. Jenkins's house. I told you not to shout," she said angrily.

"Sorry, but David and I thought it was okay," he said.

Daniela looked back for David. "But where *is* David?" she asked. "Can you see him?"

Tyler replied, "No, I can't. I hope he's okay."

They waited for David to come down the hill. But he did not come.
"Do you think David's okay?" asked Daniela.
"I don't know. It's nearly ten minutes now. What's he doing?" asked Tyler.
Then they saw the dogs on the hill. "Can you see the dogs?" asked Daniela. She pointed at the dogs on the hill.
"Oh no!" said Tyler. "I hope they don't find David!"
Daniela said, "Maybe David's in trouble!"

Daniela said, "Let's wait here. David will come back soon. I don't want to meet Mr. Jenkins's dogs."
"Yeah," Tyler agreed. "If we go into Mr. Jenkins' land, we'll get into trouble. Let's wait here."
"I hope Mr. Jenkins didn't find David," said Daniela. "If he finds David, he'll be in big trouble. Old Mr. Jenkins will be very angry with him."
"Yes," said Tyler. "So we must find him. And we must find your bag."
They waited and waited for David, but he did not come back.

"We can't wait here. He's not coming. Let's go and find David," said Tyler. "I'm going to look for him."
Daniela was worried. "But Tyler, it's dangerous! There are dogs, remember?"
"Well, maybe," he said. "But David needs our help. The dogs are looking for him. Let's find him first. And we must get your bag."
Daniela and Tyler looked for David. They were frightened but decided to go.

Together, they slowly walked up the hill. Soon Daniela found her bag. "Oh, no. My camera's broken," she said.
Tyler saw something and said, "Daniela, come and look at this."
"What is it, Tyler?" she asked.
"It's blood," he said.
"Blood?" said Daniela. "David's blood?"
Daniela said, "This is terrible. I think the dogs found David. He's hurt. We should try to find him and take him to the hospital."

They walked through the trees. Tyler said, "Here's some more blood. Look! Let's go this way." He pointed through the trees. They walked a little more and then Daniela saw something.
"What's this?" she asked.
"They're dogs' footprints," said Tyler. "And here's some more of David's blood, too! David was here!"
"Let's go and find him," he said.
"But the dogs . . ." she replied.
Tyler replied, "Okay, let's stay away from Mr. Jenkins's dogs."

They walked a little more. Then Daniela heard a noise. "Did you hear that?" she asked.
"Yeah," said Tyler. "The noise is coming this way."
Then Daniela saw a man and his big, strong dogs coming down the hill. "It's Mr. Jenkins and his dogs. Let's run away," she said.
Tyler replied, "No, the dogs will hear us! Go behind that tree, and be quiet."
"But the . . ." said Daniela.
Daniela and Tyler ran behind the tree as quietly as they could. Soon, Mr. Jenkins and the dogs came to them. They were very close.

Tyler put his hand over her mouth. "Shh!" he said.
"Don't speak. I hope the dogs don't find us!"
"Please dogs, don't find us," thought Daniela. "Please."
Daniela was very worried. She did not want the dogs to find them. Tyler was very worried, too. He thought about David's blood. He thought about the signs.
"Go away quickly," he thought.

Soon, Mr. Jenkins and the dogs went down the hill.
Daniela and Tyler watched them.
"Quick, let's go and find David," said Tyler quietly. "But be quiet."
Daniela said, "I don't want to go," she said. "I'm going back home."
"Then go down the hill by yourself," said Tyler. "The dogs are down there. I'm going to look for David."
"Okay, okay, I'm coming," she replied.
They both walked up the hill to look for David. Then they heard another noise.

"What's that? It's another noise," said Daniela. "It's coming from those trees. Maybe it's some more dogs. Quick, get behind that tree." Tyler and Daniela ran behind the tree.
A little bird came out of the tree and walked on the path.
"It's only a bird," said Tyler. "We're scared of birds now," he laughed.
"Be quiet!" said Daniela. "Or the dogs will hear us."

Soon they saw old Mr. Jenkins's house. It looked very scary. "I don't like that house," said Tyler.

"Maybe Mr. Jenkins caught David," said Daniela. "He may be in that house. Mr. Jenkins is not here now, he's down the hill. Let's go inside."

"Good thinking, Daniela," said Tyler. "Let's go and look."

They went to the house slowly. There were many signs saying *Keep out* and *Stay away.*

"I don't like this place," said Daniela.

"Yeah! I hope there are no more big dogs," replied Tyler.

Soon they got to Mr. Jenkins's house. The house looked very old. It was dark. It did not look very safe.
Daniela said, "I think something is wrong here. It's a very strange place."
"Can you see any dogs?" asked Tyler.
"No, I can't, but there are many footprints," replied Daniela. "Where's David? Is he here?"
Then Tyler saw some more blood. "Look, the blood goes into the house," he said.
"Maybe David's inside," said Daniela.

Slowly, Tyler and Daniela went up to the house. They were very nervous. They looked everywhere for more dogs.

"Be quiet, Daniela," said Tyler. "We don't want the dogs to hear us."

"Look, there's the door," said Daniela. "You go first."

"Me?" replied Tyler. "Me? Why me? I don't like dogs either."

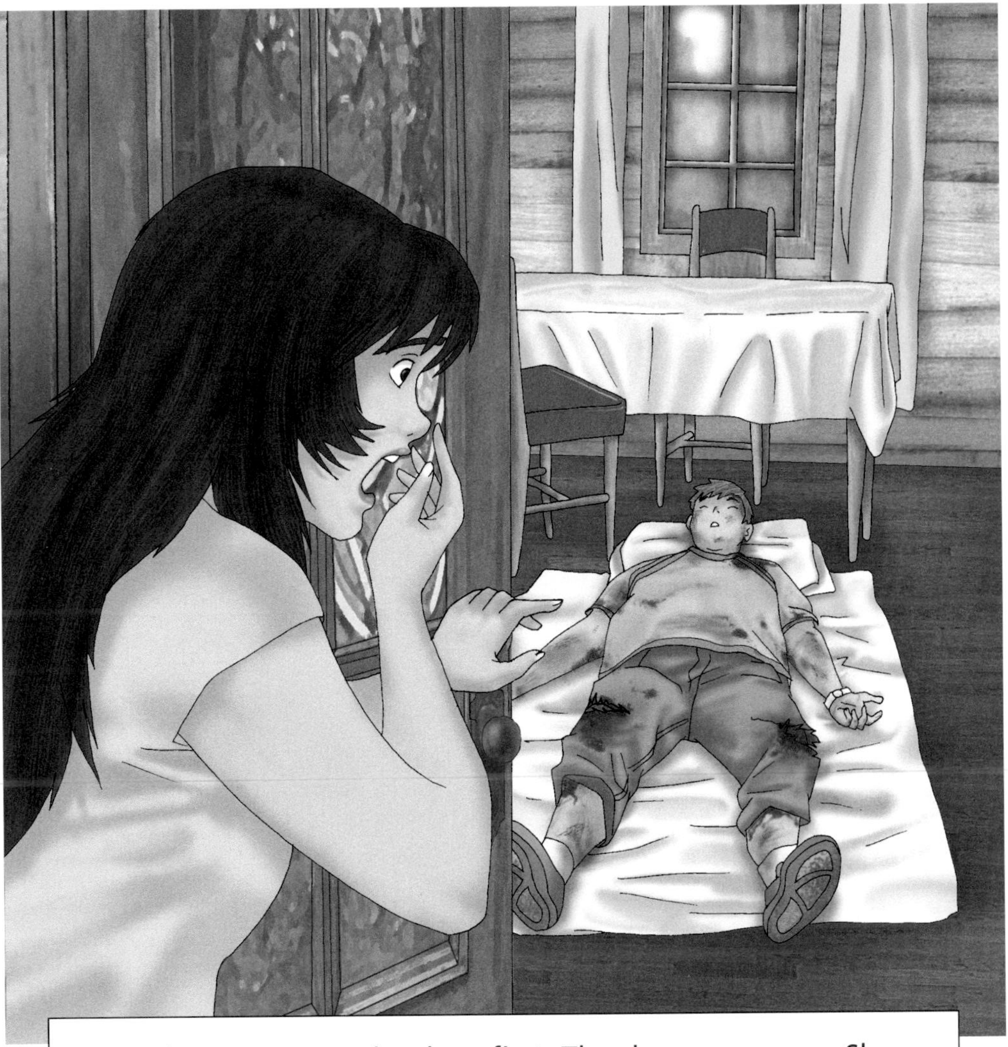

Daniela went up to the door first. The door was open. She looked inside.
Daniela thought, "Oh no! Oh no!" She put her hands to her mouth. She was so shocked, she could not say anything.
"What's wrong?" asked Tyler. "Are there some more dogs?"
"No," she replied. "It's David. He's dead."
Tyler looked at David. "What?" he said. They were both really shocked.

Daniela and Tyler went quietly into the house. They were very scared. Daniela thought, "Maybe Mr. Jenkins will come back and catch us, too?"
They walked to David and looked at him. There was blood all over him. He was not moving.
Daniela said quietly, "Oh, no. David's dead. Let's tell the police."
"Daniela," Tyler said quietly. "Yes, let's get out of here, before it's too late." They turned and went back to the door.

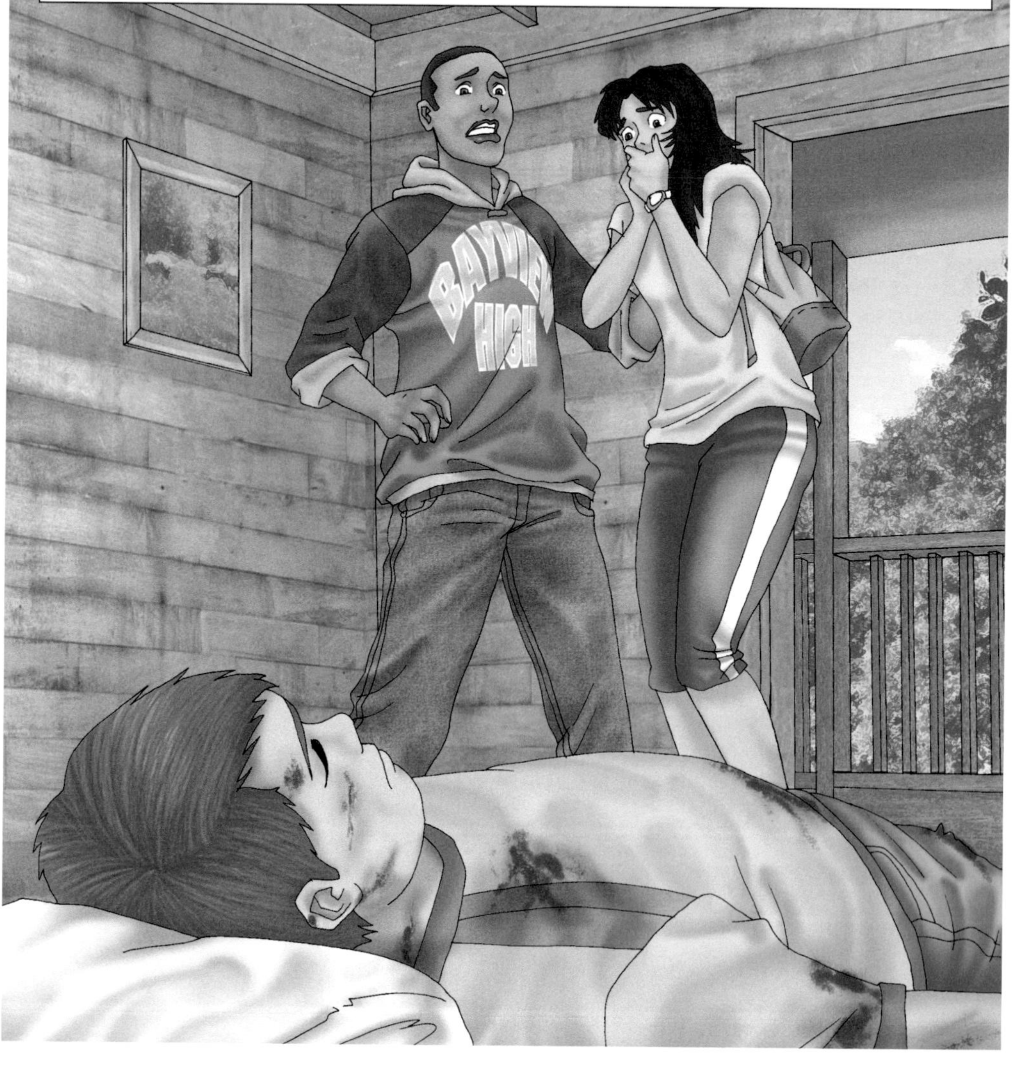

Just then, two big, angry dogs came in the door. They looked very, very angry.
"Ahhhhhh . . . !" Daniela screamed. It made the dogs more angry.
The dogs slowly walked up to Tyler and Daniela. They barked at them. Daniela and Tyler walked back into the room. They could not get out of the door.
"What do we do?" said Tyler. "What do we do? We're going to die! I'm too young to die!"
Tyler and Daniela were very scared. Daniela screamed again.

Suddenly, Mr. Jenkins came in the door. "Away!" he said to the dogs. The dogs went away. They stopped being angry.
"I guess, you're Daniela, and you're Tyler, right?" said Mr. Jenkins.
Tyler and Daniela were very shocked. "How does he know our names?" they thought.
"Your friend David is safe," he said. "He's badly hurt. But he's okay. He fell off his bike. My dogs found him and I brought him here."
Daniela looked at Tyler. They were very surprised. Then they heard, "Daniela? Tyler? Where am I?"

"David! You're not dead!" cried Daniela. She was very happy. "I was so worried about you! Are you okay?"
"No," he replied. "But Mr. Jenkins says I'll be okay soon."
Tyler said, "Thank you for helping David, Mr. Jenkins."
"You were very lucky, David," said Daniela. "You were lucky Mr. Jenkins saw you."
David replied, "No, it was his dogs. They found me. They're very smart." David told them what happened. "I fell off my bike. Then I heard the dogs barking. Then Mr. Jenkins came. He brought me here."

Daniela and Tyler stayed at Mr. Jenkins's house for a long time. Soon David was better. Mr. Jenkins gave them some drinks. They liked Mr. Jenkins now. He was friendly, and his dogs were very friendly, too.

They were sitting at the table when Mr. Jenkins asked, "Where were you going?"

"We were going to the beach," replied Daniela. "Then David and Tyler saw your dogs. We got scared and ran away and David got hurt."

"Many people are scared of my dogs. They don't like strangers," said Mr. Jenkins. "That's good because I don't want people to come here."

"Why, Mr. Jenkins?" asked Tyler.

Mr. Jenkins thought for a long time. He looked sad. Then he said, "I live here alone. For a long time, I wanted people to stay away from here. I was born in this house. My father told me to keep people away. He didn't want people to find out our secret. But now I'm old. Now you are here, I must tell you my family's secret."

"Secret?" asked Daniela. "What secret?"

"Can you keep the secret?" Mr. Jenkins asked them.

"Of course," they all said. "What is it?"

Mr. Jenkins smiled and said, "Then if you can promise, come with me and I'll show you my friends."

"Friends?" asked Tyler.

Everybody went to the front of the house.
"There! I want to show you my dolphins," Mr. Jenkins said.
There were some dolphins playing at the beach. "They live here at Jenkins Beach. I take care of the dolphins. I don't want people to know about them. I want them to be safe."
They enjoyed watching the dolphins for a long time.
Daniela said excitedly, "Wow! They're so nice. Are they yours?"
"Yes, they are my dolphins. Well, I think so," Mr. Jenkins replied.
"They are very important to me. Let's go and meet them."